King of the Rug

Written by Clare Helen Welsh

Illustrated by Patricia Grannum

Collins

Will is fed up.

2

Will gets in a ship.

Jax pulls Will off the rug.

The ship sinks.

Will gets on the bunk bed.

Will pulls Jax up.

The dog is king of that rug!

/j/

14

🐾 Review: After reading 🐾

Use your assessment from hearing the children read to choose any GPCs, words or tricky words that need additional practice.

Read 1: Decoding

- Ask the children to read page 2. Encourage them to blend in their heads as they read these words. Focus on the meaning of **fed up**. Ask: How do people feel when they are fed up? (e.g. *sad, bored*)
- On page 6, ask the children to find the word that ends in the /ng/ sound. (***king***) On page 10, can they find the word that ends in /nk/? (***bunk***) Ask them to read these words ending in "nk" and "ng":

  pink   ink   thank   ring   song   long

- Look at the "I spy sounds" pages (14–15) together. Ask the children to point out as many things as they can find in the picture that begin with the /j/ sound. (e.g. *jet, juice, Jax, jumper, jaguar, juggling, jam on toast*)

Read 2: Prosody

- Turn to pages 8 and 9 and model reading with a storyteller voice. Ask the children to read the pages themselves, encouraging them to think about the tones they use to make the story sound exciting. Ask:
  - What tone could you use for page 8? (e.g. *surprised, dramatic*)
  - How do you want the reader to feel? (e.g. *worried, nervous*)
  - What tone could you use for Jax? (e.g. *loud, urgent*) Why? (e.g. *Jax is scared and anxious*)
- Ask the children to take turns to read the pages dramatically to the class.

Read 3: Comprehension

- Encourage the children to describe imaginary places they go to while playing. Talk about any items they use to make pretend places, such as the underneath of a table for a cave or pillows for a castle.
- Talk about the ordinary things that become important parts of Will and Jax's imaginary adventure. Ask:
  - What does the basket become? (*a ship*)
  - What does the rug become? (*an island*)
  - What scary thing is the dog in the adventure? (*a shark*)
  - Why was the dog the king at the end? (*it sat on the rug, and the rug was the island*)